1

The Living Contradiction: Analyses of US internal imperial system

Table of Contents

Intro

This book is dedicated to Canek Sanchez Guevara, the grandson of Che Guevara, who corresponded with me for several years and passed away in Mexico at the age of 40 in early 2015. Outliving his grandfather by a year, Canek was a prolific writer in Europe and Central America, as well as his last place of exile, Mexico, where his grandfather had also gone (Canek was born in Cuba and lived there till the 90s). Canek was the name given to the descendants of the Maya who were warriors who resisted the Spanish for some time, especially in Guatemala, where Che was as well. Canek Sanchez Guevara wrote against totalitarianism and continued the legacy of his grandfather fighting injustice. Who better to honor when writing of imperialism?

In a way I honor Che as well, a firm anti imperialist who sacrificed his life for the cause. Usually when people talk of imperialism they are talking about the external arm rather than the internal, how the US has backed repressive fascist military juntas, especially in Latin America, as well as intervened in nations. However, I am going to analyze how internally the US has set up an imperial system separating people by social class, race and gender, in order to divide and conquer, just as the US does to other weaker nations of the "third world". The US principally uses media propaganda to encourage this divide. However, US corporate control over media is failing as alternative media comes about and a counter culture is set up, which is going beyond a sub-culture.

I have written often of revolution at home, and through my activism, strived to bring this about. But as the Chinese philosophers believe, to fight your enemy you must know your enemy. From the empire of the US, the largest empire in history with more outposts or bases than any empire in history, and the only empire to deny being an empire. We see the living contradiction, in a society that proposes to be the most free in the world. To fight this contradiction we must properly understand it, and find the right course or tactic to take on this injustice. Bernie Sanders reformism will not lead us to a "political revolution". Limiting ourselves to the confines of chauvinist nationalist thinking will get us nowhere. We need an actual revolution and to coordinate this with leaders not false prophets, as I have warned about in previous books. And so we will delve into the reality of the living contradiction.

Al R Suarez

October 10th, 2015

Tampa, Fl

Chapter I   Propaganda

The term propaganda used to mean nothing but information. Ministers of Propaganda gave info without the slightest bit of negative connotation. It was not till WWII that the word started to be associated with lies or deceptions, such as Nazi propaganda. The CIA, started in 1948, in one of their first programs, did Operation Paperclip, which recruited many high ranking Nazis and learned many of the propaganda tactics from the Nazis which was later implemented in American society. Those recruited included "the butcher of Lyon" Klaus Barbie, who headed the Lyon concentration camp in France and was wanted in Europe. He emerged in Bolivia and helped train the rangers who killed Che Guevara. He was part of the "cocaine coup" that overthrew a Bolivian government. He may have been one of the Nazis Che's father sent in his youth to spy on the exiled Nazis in Cordoba, Argentina, as Che's father was a anti-fascist activist.

Not just Argentina and Bolivia, but Paraguay was known to be a haven for escaped Nazi war criminals, who became advisers in the junta governments, especially in the 70s during "the condor years". It should be noted the policy of harboring Nazis was fully supported by Kissinger (Secretary of State under Nixon), who emigrated to the US to escape the Nazis and had fought Nazis during WWII, but helped Nazis when the Cold War culminated. Klaus was not sent back to Europe till Che was already long dead, a holocaust survivor went to Bolivia and pressured the government there to reveal his real identity, when the Bolivian government changed they sent him to justice. I will get into more details on this in the next chapter.

The famous quote from the Nuremberg Trials by the Nazi war criminal Goring said in 1947 comes to mind when I think of propaganda "The people can always be brought to the bidding of the leaders. That is easy. All you have to do is tell them they are being attacked and denounce the pacifists for lack of patriotism and exposing the country to danger. It works the same way in any country". This quote is at least famous in some circles as people still have not learned the valuable lessons from the war.

Chapter 2 External Imperialism

In order to understand internal imperialism which tends to be covert, we must understand the history of US external imperialism which is more overt. US interventions, especially in Latin America, culminated by the early 1950s with the US backed coup against the progressive Guatemalan leader Jacobo Arbenz, of which Che himself was a witness. Am going to start this chapter sharing a recent article I wrote on this topic from my facebook notes.

42 Years Since The US Backed Reign of Terror Started In South America, The Latin's 911

September 11, 2015 at 11:00am

Friends ▼

By Al Suarez

I used to write a note every couple weeks its been at least a month since I've written one. A lot has been going on. This is my first note since I disassociated from Chris. I kept my manifesto I wrote him with him in notes for prosterity. Am now doing a new program with Luciano called Peurvian Rebel Radio. But it is not my intention today to talk about that in this article. I am now going to delve into a topic Americans are generally ignorant about. The infamous Condor Years at the height of the Cold War, which happened throughout the 70s where neo nazi (literally nazis wanted in Europe were being advisers to the regimes with help from the CIA) and fascist military juntas were propped up all over South America backed by Nixon, Kissinger & Co. Peru was one of the few countries that did not have a coup, and took in many refugees under the government of Velasco, my father was living in his native Peru at the time in his 20s. It all started on September 11th, 1973. The democratically elected Socialist Salvador Allende, was being bombed in La Moneda presidential palace, in Santiago, Chile, after three years in power where he made radical changes to help the peasants, students and working class of his nation, inspiring movements throughout Latin America and the world. He gave a farewell address on the radio, and then using the rifle Fidel gave him on a trip to Chile, shot himself. It was thought he may have died resisting the fascists entering the palace, but an autopsy decades later confirmed it was a suicide. Allende contributed much to the revolution even before becoming president, he was a friend of Che Guevara and as governor of a province of northern Chile took in the survivor's of Che's campaign in Bolivia and helped them escape.

Unlike Hugo Chavez, who they tried to do a coup against in 2002, Allende did not have the allies in the military he needed to survive, and his revolution was peaceful in violent times. General Pinochet the traitor and fascist, took over, and an era of brutal repression, death camps, and persecution ensued, many went into exile, including Allende's niece Isabel Allende who would later move from journalism to becoming a great author inspired by Pablo Neruda, many called her later the female Garcia Marquez. Many films were made based off of Isabel's novels, where known actors played like Antonio Banderas. Garcia Marquez himself and many revolutionary authors throughout the world knew President Allende, Garcia Marquez also had many films made after his novels, where actors like Javier Bardem played, authors and poets such as Eduardo Galeano who passed away earlier this year (as Garcia Marquez did in 2014, only not in exile in Mexico away from his native Colombia, but Galeano died in his homeland of Uruguay, where his friend Mujica took power) were also influenced by Allende. The Venezuelan singer known as Ali Primera also made songs about Allende, including after the coup.

Victor Jara became one of the 10,000 Chilean citizens killed at the hands of the fascists, he was one of the musical revolutionary artists who could not get away, and he was tortured to death in a Chilean concentration camp dying September 15th 1973. US imperialism was directly responsible for his death and all the regimes came about in their terror in countries like Bolivia, Argentina and Paraguay. In the 80s as well Central America had its share of US backed fascist regimes who countered the Sandinista revolution in Nicaragua. Today the legacy of Allende is strong, we see Nicaragua, Venezuela, Ecuador, Bolivia, Argentina, all countries ruled by left or center left democratic presidents who have united with each other against fascism and US imperialism like never before, using their resources to better the conditions of the poor, working class and indigenous people of their nations in particular. This gives hope for the rest of the world in the struggle, especially in southern Europe where countries like Spain and Greece are under pressure from the IMF, well the Latins have experience in dealing with IMF and were able to defeat the economic imperialists in their territory, an example for all oppressed people who were able to become free, because of the huge sacrifice of great people like Salvador Allende. His first name means savior, and he really was a savior to a lot of people, we shall never forget...

Last image taken of Allende, taken during the bombing of the palace, shortly before his farewell address on the radio, and rather than be captured and tortured, he shot himself with honor.

Indeed, leaders like Allende and Arbenz, both connected to Che Guevara, were prime examples of men considered threats to the US empire, but who's ousting from power turned them into heroes to the Latin people. Zelaya and Lugo are but recent examples In a long list of Latin American leaders ousted by US imperialism. Even former allies of the US, like Noriega, later turned into enemies, which is reminiscent of when Saddam was a friend of the US than foe, or Bin Laden, yet Bin Laden never headed the government in Afghanistan, as he was Saudi in origin. Could Che however, an Argentine, have headed the government in Bolivia? I don't see why not, Bolivia which was Upper Peru when it was in the Spanish empire, is a country named after a Venezuelan (Simon Bolivar). Che's full name was Ernesto Rafael Guevara Lynch de la Serna, his mother was ironically a descendant of Jose de la Serna, part of the Argentine aristocracy, who was the last Viceroy of Spain, defeated in the battle of Ayacucho by Bolivar's second in command Sucre, a Venezuelan who left his post in Ecuador to help fulfill Bolivar's plan in Peru, and who had Upper Peru renamed. This was an extension of the liberator Bolivar's plan in Grand Colombia (modern day Panama, Colombia and Venezuela).

Later Jose Marti, the apostle of Cuban independence, a poet who had been persecuted for his activism against the Spanish empire, an admirer of Bolivar, attempted his own anti Spanish imperialist struggle in Cuba, which was one of the last bastions of the Spanish empire. Marti lived in exile in the US including here in Tampa, and knew when the Spanish left the North Americans would try to impose their will as well, which came in the form of the Monroe Doctrine. Marti had traveled to Venezuela to know the land of his hero. Bolivarianism was reborn in the early 2000s with the election of Hugo Chavez and his successive elections thereafter in Venezuela itself, which formed alliance and integrated with the rest of

Latin America, including most of South America, for a time Honduras and Nicaragua, as the relationship with Nicaragua continues as the only Central American leftist government. Maduro, Venezuela's president since the death of Chavez, is continuing a similar policy of integration, Socialism and anti-imperialism.

Chapter 3 Internal Imperialism

What is not often looked at or discussed is the internal consequences for large sections of the US populace as a result of the imperialist policies of the government. Men accused of being tyrants from Napoleon to Stalin have been the scapegoats for those societies and how history has judged them, in the US it is not necessarily one particular man you can blame, the system is rigged against third parties, and the elites ultimately control who will run in the two Capitalist parties.

The first way internal imperialism is felt is in how the poor is treated, especially people of color of the "lower classes". A nation should always be judged on how it treats its most vulnerable. The downtrodden, the homeless, who were the weaker people that Hitler rounded up and put in camps before others. In fact the Jews had economic power in Germany and were not put into ghettos till much later. And these were not the first ghettos. People say ghetto in the US to refer to "darker neighborhoods" where usually poor people of color live, and where crime can be a problem, including drug use or selling. But who invented the ghetto? Who brought the drugs? We will get into that. The first ghetto was the Venetian Ghetto which became famous through Shakespeare's The Merchant of Venice. Jews were not allowed outside the gates of the ghetto without wearing a red cap signifying they were not Christian. Jews were discriminated against and spat on in the city state.

The ghetto or "hood" as we know it was invented by the US government. When the Black Panther Party for Self Defense was infiltrated from the fed's COINTELPRO program, crack cocaine was used to split the remaining factions of those panthers who were not in jail or killed. I described in prior books how this program was used to infiltrate other movements such as Occupy. They turned out to be the gangs of the bloods and the crips who were well funded and armed. The panthers gained momentum after the death of their inspirer Malcolm X in the late 60s, by the late 70s they were falling apart, and in the 80s the crack era came in with gang warfare dividing up the black and brown communities in the urban areas of the country such as in LA and Detroit.

Tupac Shakur, who came from the prominent Shakur family of the panthers, was a gang member at one time, his mother was a political prisoner who was released since she was pregnant with him. Tupac Amaru Shakur was named after the Inca warrior Tupac Amaru, who fought the Spanish in Peru, and a couple centuries later a descendant, who went by the title Tupac Amaru II also led a rebellion against Spanish rule, this helped leave the seeds of a rebellion that would start soon have he sacrificed his life as well, with Bolivar, as ending slavery and fighting for indigenous rights was essential to his anti-imperialist fight. What the Peruvian priest Gustavo Gutierrez would later call liberation theology, the natives had some support from progressive elements of the Church in the tradition of Barolome de las Casas who convinced the Spanish crown to make native slavery illegally (it still happened, the Portuguese were complicit, and blacks were brought in, natives were dying off anyway from disease in large numbers when in contact with Spanish). Many of these progressives were Jesuits, and Jesuits were subsequently exiled from Latin America. The current Pope was a Jesuit.

In the time of Bolivar in the early 19th century, the Haitians recently defeating Napoleon II, had helped Bolivar in exchange for a promise to end slavery in the lands that would be liberated. In the US 5 de Mayo is celebrated as an important date for Mexican Americans, what a lot of Americans don't realize is that is actually not their independence day, it is the day the Mexicans in the battle of Puebla defeated the troops of Napoleon II as well. This helped bring about an end to the era of the Bonaparte family, as Napoleon II's uncle was the originator and was defeated in Waterloo. If you look at the history of the Caesars, it is quite similar, Caesar Augustus being the nephew of Julius Caesar.

Back to Tupac Shakur, his mother's stepsister, Assata Shakur, was also a political prisoner and was able to escape jail after being framed, and subsequently went into exile in Cuba. It will be interesting to see if this will be a sticking point in the negotiations with Cuba during the "normalization" as essentially this is not a lifting of the US economic embargo, and Obama, following orders as a good house slave, has done what white presidents have failed to do since Miss Shakur was wanted in the 70s, put her up to the top of the FBI most wanted list. At least the rest of the Cuban 5 political prisoners were sent back to Cuba, but Mumia, Peltier, and others, whether Native American or fighters for black liberation, continue to be behind US bars. An entire generation of revolutionaries remain in the prison industrial complex, which Michelle Alexander refers to as the New Jim Crow showing how the for profit prisons have slavery and are filled with so-called minorities. I say so-called as most of the world is not white, and we must be internationalist in scope.

So I have revealed how external imperialism and internal imperialism work, but how do we fight on two fronts both these regressive policies and its cultural implications? Building a counter culture, a movement to combat this. And this means a strong opposition to oppose the imperial forces. This will be discussed in the next chapter.

Chapter 4 Building The Opposition

To organize or form the left opposition (similar to the Left Opposition Trotsky formed against Stalin, only one that will work and unite many factions) to internal imperialism in all its forms, as I am referring to domestic opposition, what the US government calls "domestic terrorists" even if non-violent in their methods, fearing more activists rather than lone gun nuts who have done school shootings, movie theater shootings, etc, we must know the reality. And reality shows dictatorial powers have been given to the president with the introduction of laws like the Patriot Act or NDAA, under the guise of an "emergency" much like it was under the Nazi Enabling Act which gave Hitler such powers. Posting everything out in the open in social media with such laws, where people are thrown in jail for "threatening posts" in Orwellian fashion, while the society claims to be for free speech, and people like Snowden who show the truth are called traitor and forced into exile, is stupid, we must be discreet in what we post publicly and adapt when needed.

We must be tough, an individual can have redeeming qualities, but when the system is monstrous we must deal with it harshly. The term desperate times calls for desperate measures in some contexts is quite true, however should not be used to justify an injustice. A person for example who is a mercenary of the State has lost their soul and cannot be trusted. However, a person of conscious like Snowden, in-spite of being of a military background, is part of this contradiction, and went against what was taught to him sacrificing his comfortable life in Hawaii to do what was right. And for this he has earned much sympathy even from Americans. But we need to turn this into empathy, which is a different matter. Sympathy is only one step away from apathy, empathy is actually putting yourself in that person's position and feeling the rage they feel for that injustice, and in fact wanting to do something about it, and using that rage in a constructive way to do just that, and ideally, working with others in that endeavor.

The first phase is the rebellion phase than the revolutionary phase, a what Che called foco group of cadres, can work together as a vanguard, of mostly young people, to bring radical transformative change. Older generations have failed us and we see this failure in the environment, we can learn from the past but also make new methods to deal with these ongoing issues. Am now going to share my note on the question of rebellion and revolution.

Rebellion & Revolution

September 14, 2015 at 11:42pm

Am going to share some brief thoughts on these two factors. Many see these two forces as one opposing another. Others see them as one and the same. I see them as neither. Rebellion is the first phase, or should be the first phase, towards a revolutionary movement. And a movement as such must be organized. Rebellion is experimenting, often in an unorganized way, the preparation to a revolutionary scenario, or that is at least the intent of the leaders of the rebellion who are comprised primarily of youth and are a vanguard being an example to the rest as the masses will follow.

Often we hear the term rebel used generously, such as Syrian or Libyan rebels, who are often foreign and often agents of Western imperialism using the "Arab Spring" to destroy progressive nations and take their natural resources, such as oil and the like. A rebel to me is someone who is on their path towards being a revolutionary, which Che called the highest of the human species. It is a process, no revolutionary leader is born, and those that want to lead must acquire team work and self sacrifice to be that needed example in the revolutionary struggle...

Revolutionaries do not divide, they unite, they inspire, they do not incite, to incite is negative in connotation, as to incite riot, but to inspire organized resistance is another matter altogether. Let us analyze the conspiratorial, and not theorize, and put into practice revolutionary action as the consequence of rebellion can show, then and only then can we learn and adapt to set conditions for the revolution itself. As in my third book (which is now at the working class price of 5 bucks) on the revolutionary vanguard I will later go into the essence of revolution and how in context rebellion should work, and how reform is not the way.

As I described earlier in the book, reformism is not the way, in fact it is quite destructive, and in the end things will tend to go back as to where they were, with no permanent revolutionary change which needs to be radical in nature. This radicalism can be maintained through solidarity...

Chapter 5 Solidarity

The importance of solidarity had been dealt with in my prior books but I think it is one we should keep looking at and if need be redefine and examine in its proper way. The basis of solidarity is indeed empathy. Depending on parliamentary Socialism with how the system is set up in Europe (EU), and who knows in Britain and Spain by the time this is published, the situations could have changed dramatically there, can be problematic, and the leaders need to do something drastic to change this, hence the Greek situation. Before getting into the importance of empathy and fighting for the poor and working class against the bourgeois oppression; am going to share my article on the Greek situation after Tsipras's retreat giving into the principally German bankers demands, whom I have described as financial Nazis or financial terrorists and many progressive thinkers have stated the same.

I remain in solidarity with the Greek people in this crisis and hope that elements of Syriza or former Syriza members can get together to reverse this capitalization, as more and more things are happening there, such as the refugee problem and the problem of fascist groups like Golden Dawn. I have marched with Greek comrades and hold them in the highest esteem as democracy itself originated from this country.

Message To The Greek Workers

July 21, 2015 at 7:31am

Tsipras is not a traitor but unfortunately a political coward. The fact he gave in to most of the demands of the financial terrorists and passed the proposal to your parliament, makes the fact of his political cowardice undeniable, the faster this is recognized the better. Nevertheless, unlike what conspiracy theorists are saying, realistically it is my belief he was well intended but ultimately gave into pressure. Also his life was probably threatened. But if you enter revolutionary politics you have to be prepared to die, Allende in Chile in his time knew the risk he was taking, and his suicide address on the radio, recently confirmed as a suicide in an autopsy, having not died fighting the fascists entering the palace, but not giving them the satisfaction in being able to kill or torture him, but to die honorably. This address he gave probably was prepared in advance as well.

It is now time to implement measures in your country and throughout Europe to prevent the proposal from becoming a reality, which would wreck what is left of your economy, the recommendations of Comrade Costas of Syriza must be taken into account including having a default on the loan, the time for negotiations is over. Am sure you know what this proposal does, you do not need to be told this, neither by someone here in America or anywhere else. Am sure you are tired of foreigners telling you what to do, with the German Nazis of today wearing business suites attacking what is left of your country and hypocritically talking of democracy and union while they do it. In 1953 the German debt to Europe for its invasion and destruction of its people was forgiven, this included the debt Germany had with Greece which exceeds the current debt, those that bring up this debt for reparation should be paid anyway, Germany rejects, as Germany now a rich European nation, does not want to pay what it owes to a grand part of Europe. According to German logic invading a country is forgivable, but taking a loan when in need and not being able to pay it back is not.

Images have recently resurfaced of Merkel in her youth meeting with a Neo Nazi group, her country and many others clearly support Neo Nazi groups today in Ukraine, groups that were only a few years ago condemned by the EU, but which the EU, on orders from Washington, ignores its dependency on Russia for oil and supports these groups to counter Russian influence in Ukraine, but Ukraine has always had Russians living in it, and short of genocide I do not see them being kicked out, as the resistance there to the fascist government in Kiev continues, and Ukraine has been able to stay out of the Euro Zone.

The election of Syriza was historic, and symbolically against the financial terrorists of the IMF, and all its organizations which are fronts and are a fraud to do financial gangsterism against your people, taking advantage of mistakes made by your previous government who deceived the people but not the financial terrorists who knew exactly what they were doing giving those loans, as they had done prior in Latin America before the left democratic revolutions happened there of the past 16 years, culminating in the election of Hugo Chavez in 1998, and reelections of Chavez who united the continent in the name of Socialism and Simon Bolivar, the man who helped liberate grand part of the continent by Spanish imperialism, as American imperialism now in Latin America is failing. One of the first things Chavez did was help end the debt Argentina had with the IMF. We see today with the solidarity of all nations south of the US in this hemisphere condemning Obama's sanctions against the democratic government of Venezuela, even nations that claim to be allies of the US.

The downing of the plane of indigenous leader and president of Bolivia, Evo Morales, in 2013, with the complicity of Spain and Austria, who were once again, deceived by the American Empire, which Snowden had revealed prior by the fact the Empire was spying on its so-called allies in Europe, showed Europe continued to act as slave to the US, not as a equal partner. The IMF is controlled 20% by the US, therefore 20% of US taxpayers finance it, but it is ultimately controlled by American guns. The US knew Morales's plane was leaving from a different airport in Moscow where Snowden was not hiding. It was intimidation tactic to prevent Bolivia from giving him asylum, as a result not only Bolivia but Nicaragua and Venezuela offered him asylum in the end. In Spain in particular, Podemos, a new political party coming right out of the Indignado movement, we see gains in the Spanish parliament which can possibly translate to leadership in the prime ministership, which can bring hope to the Greeks and other European countries that the working class has not been forgotten, and is not alone.

After your historic referendum, 41 Syriza members of your parliament dissented from Tsipras's proposal, Comrade Zoe head of the parliament and Syriza member, gave a inspirational speech dissenting from the proposal Tsipras brought. Your former Syriza financial minister is also calling for an end to this proposal. In this defeat seeds of victory are still there. In-spite of so-called Syriza leadership giving in, many Syriza members and Anarchists of the left are hostile to the implementation of this proposal and they need to form a vanguard, and a united front, to oppose these measures. Strikes immediately need to be organized throughout Europe in solidarity with the Greek workers and students. The Greeks need to add pressure to withdraw this proposal, the Greek government needs to take steps to nationalize the banks so they belong to the public, and leaving the Euro Zone is the only option. The British government with all their hypocrisy, insists Greek stay in the euro, when they themselves have stuck to the pound currency. Out of all this the message is clear. Reformism is not the way, only through revolutionary policy and a movement backing it, can all the fears and pressures be put aside and the interests of the Greek working class be fought for, as an example to the world what the Greek people can do, who were the very people that started democracy and the concept of Europe. Greeks do not need to be told what a European is or what democracy is. German arrogance is their weakness, the German working class will soon show solidarity with the Greek, the Turkish with the Greek, etc, and these divisions will be swept away as a real democratic revolution, in the spirit of Latin America today, will spread the world over. I still remember the historic march of 2013 I took part in, in NY, including with members of Syriza in exile, where they showed solidarity with their Turkish brothers and sisters, taking off the shackles of centuries of division encouraged by governments, this unity can change the world, and must not be forgotten. We must not let the far right forces take over and take advantage of division or crisis. Revolutionary greetings from America!

In Solidarity,

Alex "Al" Suarez

Image of Greek workers protesting.

And so we go into empathy with the working class and poor, in Greece, the US, and the world over. The refugee issue has sparked much empathy as dead bodies of children refugees end up on the shores of Europe. Such empathy should also be among the US people when Central American people show up on our border many of them children and refugee. Europe was complicit in destroying Libya, and supporting rebels in Syria, which has caused much of this refugee problem, just as the US backed coup in Honduras in 2009 caused many of the problems there, and as I already mentioned there is a long history of intervention.

The US said Libya had to have a humanitarian intervention but where the humanity today? The British used Lawrence of Arabia to get rid of the Ottoman Turk control of the Middle East, and said for humanitarianism they were going after Ottoman Syria to "protect Christians". However, countries like Ethiopia, who were not a Muslim majority, wrote Italy not to colonize them since they were Christian too, and this fell on deaf ears. Religious solidarity is out the window when imperial interests are in question, only used when convenient for those with the power and might.

Am now going to share an article I wrote on a city I hold dear to my heart, Philadelphia, where the great anti imperialist document the Declaration of Independence was written, but where parts of the city is crumbling, as the US bankrupts itself funding wars and giving aid to countries like Israel who don't need it, and extend this aid to tyrants like Sisi and the Saudi crown. Another version of this article has been published in The People's Tribune out of Chicago also translated to Spanish. I hope this current book can be translated to Greek and Spanish soon, as I could do the Spanish translation myself.

The Revival in Philly: My Experience at the historic US Social Forum (26th-28th of June)

June 30, 2015 at 2:33pm

This article will be published in the People's Tribune, also to be translated to Spanish in El Tribuno del Pueblo.*

Meeting with celebrity activist rappers like Immortal Technique, and Rebel Diaz, may have been what you would expect to be the highlights of such a trip I took from Florida to Philadelphia to be at this summer's US Social Forum, however my encounters with them were brief, they were not in the march, and when you meet them, you see they are activists just like you. The encounters with them were great, but I met many extraordinary people from all over the world fighting in the same struggle for the same cause as me. I met comrades from Honduras, Peru, Montreal, Quebec, Paris, France, Ghana, Africa, from Kentucky, from Boston, from Florida, from all over, all who came to the US Social Forum to continue in their activism to bring radical revolutionary change, as I saw the revival of activism like in Occupy days come out in the great city of Philadelphia, in who's name is Greek in origin, the city of brotherly love, where the decalaration of independence was written, the hometown of Benjamin Franklin, Mumia Abu Jamal, and Noam Chomsky.

Besides those prominent names the name of Cheri Honkala should be a household name for all activists. She lives in Philly and helped revive the Poor Peoples Economic Human Rights Campaign (PPEHRC) which was started by Dr. King. She also happened to have run for vice president of the US with the Green Party in 2012. Cheri led the march we had on Saturday, along with homeless and poor people, especially people of color, some were part of the Black Lives Matter movement, others were local people Cheri was helping. People from the ghetto, from Kensington, in the area near north Philly where Temple University is, who hosted us, were present. Cheri told us the case of the 14 year old boy dying of cancer, who the Emergency Assistance people in downtown Philly has still refused to house, as they and others have not housed a single family in 5 years, as they continue to hoard tax dollars and corruption continues. That is why from north Philly we marched to their office in downtown to protest the fact families are dying on the street or being sent to the church Cheri helps run in Kensington, instead of providing the services they are paid to do. Immediately after Emergency Services we went to our final spot which was where a statue of the racist mayor of Philly from the 1970s, Mayor Rizzo, was placed, but we will get into that later.

We marched, about 500 of us, which would have been more if not for the rain, which poured at times, for a good half an hour to Emergency Services where speeches were given. Prior to that Reverend Bruce Wight went into the university where the forum was going on and on loud speaker called the comrades to come to the streets and join the march, surprisingly a large amount of the participants came out with us, including members of Code Pink. It was like God was testing our resolve, not just from the rain throughout, but as literally when we arrived at Emergency Services the rain increased and was all out pouring. In the front part of the protest there was children and people on wheelchairs throughout it, both speaking into the loud speaker along side Cheri for us to move on and what we were fighting for and started various chants, my favorite being, what was written on my sign, which I had tucked away inside my jacket most of the time as I held the PPEHRC's sign in the front, The People United Will Never Be Defeated! Or as they say in Spanish El Pueblo Unido Jamas Sera Vencido!!

The police blocked off the roads but we had our comrades in cars ahead of us, and the police who knew we never asked permission to march, parted ways and let us pass through. I felt proud we were represented as Reverend Bruce Wright, who came up from Florida with us, spoke about how Florida was one of the worse states in treating the poor and how a 93 year old man was arrested for feeding the poor in Fort Lauderdale. Bruce had walked into a workshop prior to that and asked all the comrades present who was for reform, not a single hand was raised, he then asked who was for revolution, where he got a standing ovation of people full of revolutionary enthusiasm, which showed clearly the general sentiments of the people at this particular forum, far more radical than the Left Forums I had been at prior in NY. I thought to myself as we marched how glad I was I decided not to fly back but to stay an extra day to be in the march and return to Florida with my comrades in a van. Among those to speak when we finally reached Emergency Services was an activist from my area I had not met till then, Pedro El Poeta, or Pedro the Poet, who was a rapper activist. Florida was clearly represented in that march.

We then converged on the Rizzo statue, and exposed this old mayor for his racist practices in Philly, this was the man who helped set up the black panther affiliate and activist Mumia, who is still in jail to this day. The city could have money to erect such statues but not to help the poor dying in the streets. As we marched towards Rizzo we say a huge abandoned church, which comes out in the youtube video of the forum which was already released. After a long march I finally made it back to the church in West Kensington where we had been sleeping, to see performances were being set up. Pedro El Poeta was to perform again with his incredible revolutionary energy, as he was on the frontlines of the march, barely rested, and had done a concert along side Dave his backup singer, the night before. Pedro is originally from Nicaragua, and had migrated to Florida some years prior, he also happens to be a teacher teaching troubled High School students. On the way back in the van I called into a radio program I co host and passed the phone over to Pedro so he could be interviewed. Krown Deon is a rapper activist as well, out of St. Pete, Fl who performed and did the roadtrip, I met him prior. Also the next day, this morning, I was on Don's program he co hosts out of Sarasota, Fl. Don 79 years old was also in the march. There was people of all ages and colors present. Don had in fact been to Peru where my father is from, and met Gustavo Gutierrez, the founder of Liberation Theology, Don also knew Dr. King. Right after Don interviewed me he had Bruce Wright himself call in, and we are working here to continue our work and spread the word inspired by the forum in Philly.

While I marched, it was my first major march since Occupy a couple years prior, I thought of all those who died too young, and left behind their legacy for us to fight for. I thought of Anne Frank, of my comrade Marty Droll who I had marched with in Tampa and showed me around Philly in my first trip there, and of my sister Tasha Suarez. I thought how this would inspire my third book and my continued activist work. How this vanguard of people, the downtrodden of society, could come together and make the impossible possible. The theme for the forum was Another World Is Possible, which was a common chant in Occupy. I think not only is another world possible or probable but inevitable, we can be the change, for the very survival of the human species, so that all the sacrifices before us are not in vain and our children and grandchildren can live in a better society, as they deserve better. I fight for the future of my niece and all the unborn children, as we dream for a new society and make this dream a reality. Hope to see you at the World Forum in Montreal next year!

The author in Philly just before the march

Contradiction is not always hypocritical, but may be the process of being an intellectual. Intellectuals I respect but don't always agree with like Chomsky, have said contradictory things. For example, he wrote a book called "Failed States" and most people thought he was referring to how the US is becoming a failed state. But then Chomsky stuns us with statements like the US is the freest society in the world. Or he comes out saying Obama is worse than Bush, then says if he was in a battleground state he would vote to re-elect Obama. I was so stunned by that last statement I thought the recording of him saying that was tampered with and emailed him myself as I have had correspondence, and he admitted he said that. To be fair Chomsky did support the Green Party, but then again he is not in a battleground state like Florida where the vote is important.

Also Socialist leaders in the US like Sawant of the Seattle city council, who I've seen speak, have used terms like radical reform, she is not an Orthodox Trotskyist, but Socialist Alternative are comprised of people who associate with Trotsky, who was firmly anti reform, and considered real radicalism non reformist. I respect Sawant but terms like this also are a contradiction. When I pointed this out to one of her supporters he took offense. To do an oxymoron you do not have to be a moron. Norman Finkelstein for example, talked about how Gandhi openly admitted to having contradictions. Great thinkers have done contradictions.

There are negative contradictions however, and when you take a society or system's contradictions in contrast to an individual, it could be much more serious. Bernie Sanders has voted against war, says he is against it, but at every opportunity he has financed it, he has in the Senate allocated funds for wars in Afghanistan and Iraq, and even recently voted for a billion dollar package being sent to the fascists in Ukraine who took over there, exacerbating the problem with eastern Ukraine and the Russians, as the Russians go into Syria. This is a dangerous contradiction, and seeing no viable candidate of the left, as the Democratic Party is not the Labour Party of Britain (Corbyn seems to be of the left of Tsipras, Woods & Galloway backing him says a lot), want to support him, and third parties are continually discriminated against.

The justification is that the allocations are to help the soldiers. But did Bush help finance the VA to take care of veterans, or give soldiers the proper equipment? You had cases where families sent bullet proof vests to their kids in Iraq since the government failed to provide them. To pressure the US to leave Afghanistan, unfortunately allocations need to cease, ultimately the soldiers will get out of harm's way by leaving. The US has now been in Afghanistan longer than it was in Vietnam. Afghanistan is not known as the graveyard of empires for nothing. I can get into the long history of that, but I want to stay relevant to this question of the contradictions in US society and how to deal with it.

The US claims to be an equal partner for peace in Israel/Palestine, but do nothing but continue to send aid to Israel when Netanyahu is reelected on the promise to break the two state solution. Like Chomsky I believe a two state solution as with international consensus in the UN, can happen, and it would be a step to a one state where Jews would live as a minority like before, and the refugees return, and no one is persecuted for their beliefs, under one secular state. The UN however until power is taken from the security council and countries can vote freely without coercion, will continue to be useless in maintaining international law universally. Netanyahu uses his agents in the US Congress with AIPAC lobby and corporate money, to try to sabotage the Iran deal. He then promises to call the dogs off if Obama extends the bribe or aid to Israel, which Obama is obliged to do. Who is the superpower here? The question remain on the extent of the influence of Israel over US foreign policy. And the current presidential elections has the candidates generally ignoring foreign policy issues.

This reflects the nationalist tendencies of the US public, it's on the youth in the spirit of internationalism and wanting to know foreign issues to pressure the candidates to talk on these issues, so even if they want to avoid it they will have to answer. But beyond discourse, we need action. Bernie has made chauvinist statements like immigrants take away American jobs, and this all reflects he is not a Socialist, especially his funding of empire. He is progressive on some of the domestic agenda, but on the fundamentals he is clearly to the right. The lesser of two evils justification is getting old. We see there could be a continuation of the Bush-Clinton dynasty that went on for 3 decades. Regardless of the elections, we need activism to make a difference.

Conclusion

They say a picture is worth a thousand words. Am going to end this book with a series of images, as I have not used images in my last two books (only in my first one). Each image will have a description of how that person inspires me as I am not full of myself as some authors tend to be. In my first book there was images throughout, a conclusion and then a set of images. The images will be the conclusion.

Hugo Chavez, one of my principal inspirations, a true democratic socialist, not this fake progressive like Bernie.

With the co host of my new blogtalkradio show Vanguard Youth Radio, Andrea Nordera.

Luciano de la Vega, activist rapper out of Philly, who promotes Vanguard Youth Radio.

Pedro El Poeta (Pedro The Poet) who I mentioned in the book's version of the article on the Philly trip is also a activist rapper. He had been a guest on my old show. He is in the Tampa Bay area as well.

Reverend Bruce Wright, a progressive preacher in Tampa Bay area who has gone on many road-trips with me and has been mentioned in my books.

Cheri Honkala, head of the Poor People's Economic Human Rights Campaign out of Philly, and former Vice Presidential candidate for the US 2012 with the Green Party.

Russian revolutionary Leon Trotsky

Canek Sanchez Guevara

Martin Droll AKA Comrade Marty who I dedicated my last book to, activist out of Philly who passed away last year in mysterious circumstances.